CLOSING

Category: Business & Economics

Description: Closing the sale, ask for the order and get paid.

Key words: closing the sale, closing techniques, how to close, sales closing.

Copyright Bob Oros-2017
ISBN 978-1-105-22537-6

Written and published by Bob Oros

CLOSING 1

Closing Ask for the order and get paid 5

Ask for the order 5

The direct close 7

Choice close 8

The choice set up 9

Guarantee close 12

Time advantage 13

Trial close 14

"Ask a question" close 14

Doorknob close 15

Silent close 16

The truth about closing 16

How you decide 19

Closing on price 22

After the close 24

Expect the sale..27

Closing: Ask for the order and get paid 34

My 4% improvement objective:..36

What the entire book series will do for you 38

Ben Franklin's system 39

Achieve a 52% improvement..44

Closing
Ask for the order and get paid

Ask for the order

If everything has been done correctly up to the time to close, the close will come naturally. Let's assume we lack just that final touch that puts us in the class of a "Cutting Edge" professional closer. What is that touch? First, the difference between an amateur and a professional closer are that both have the technique at hand; but the amateur uses it so crudely the buyer sees it and resents it. The professional by practice has polished his or her close to the point where it is relaxed and natural. Only one in four (25%) sales people ask for an order after a sales presentation.

Make every call with a specific objective and close on that objective. The amateur, the beginner, still suffers with the delusion that he or she has accomplished something when he just "drops in" for a friendly call. The amateur excuses their lack of closing skill by saying to him or her self, "This will help me get in solid with the buyer." The amateur claims that the call has a lot of advertising value even though they made the call without a specific objective. They do not know that 20% of the sales people on the force take 80% of the orders because they know how to close; that only one in four has a specific call objective and closes on that objective.

To permit the buyer to defer the close is to leave the sale OPEN to a competitor. The Cutting-Edge professional KNOWS that it never pays to leave business on the table. You know that to permit the buyer to defer the close is to leave the sale OPEN to a competitor to walk in and take the harvest when you has planted and worked the crop. The sales person who has polished the technique of closing to professional brilliance knows the fundamental difference between so-called "high pressure" selling and "low pressure". You know the value of intelligent, dramatic, forceful, suggestive closing when you feel in your heart you are rendering a great service by helping the buyer to decide something for the buyer's own good.

You are in the strong position because you have the advantage of working with an organized plan and objective. After all, every sale is a contest, starting with two strikes on the buyer, because you have the advantage of working with an organized plan and an objective toward which you are steering him or her. The buyer is in the weak position of a follower on the defensive. The Cutting-edge professional has learned by sad experience that failure to close, to permit the decision to be deferred lets the prospect get cold, when they might have been sold by the application of a quiet, smooth-running closing technique.

The direct close

The direct close is one of the best ways to close because you get it over with up front and there is no doubt about what you are there for. We literally start the presentation with the close. One thing that is extremely important in using this tactic is you have to know exactly what you want before making the call. An example: "I would like to have your ham business, what do I need to do to get it?" "I would like to have your produce business, what would my company and I have to do to get it?"

Choice close

The choice close is the most common close, however, it is often incorrectly used. If we wait until the end of the presentation and then try and squeeze the customer into a corner they will resent it. The correct way to use this tactic is to build it into your presentation by offering two or three different choices, explaining all the differences as well as the features and benefits of each product, and let them choose the one that best fits their needs. For example we could bring three different hams to a customer; a buffet ham, a PIT ham and a football ham. As we were making the presentation we would point out the advantages and disadvantages of each product, letting them make the final decision. The theory behind this close is that we give them a choice between something and something else and let them make the choice. We never want to give them a choice between something and nothing. This close is especially good for the "price buyer". We can show the low quality product, the middle quality product and the high quality product, pointing out that the higher price is really going to cost less in the long run.

The choice set up

What's the difference between the choice close and the choice set up?

I am at the airport and the flight I am waiting to board is oversold. The attendant jokingly offers to pay $5,000 to anyone who is willing to give up their seat. He immediately admits that he was kidding and says he will pay $200 if anyone would be willing to give up their seat and take a later flight. No takers! Why? He misused the choice close set up. If he would have jokingly offered $25 and then raised it to $200 it would have seemed like a real deal.

Nearly everyone in sales knows how to use the choice close; what day would you like delivery, Tuesday or Wednesday? What pack size would be best for you, 12 or 24? You ask the customer to choose between something you want and something else you want and them make the choice – you win both ways. Now let's take it to a higher level by including the element of contrast. Give them a choice between something they don't want and something they didn't know they wanted until you presented the choice.

Let's say you are going to sell a house to a prospective buyer. The price you want is $100,000. You first take them to a $125,000 house that is overpriced by $25,000. Next you take them to a $75,000 house in need of $50,000 worth of repairs located in a poor area. NOW you take them to your perfectly priced house - $100,000. The choice for the buyer is clear.

How about the used car sales person? They first show you an old clunker that is overpriced and barely runs. Next they show you the car they really want to sell you. In your mind you are comparing the differences and thinking about what a great bargain it is!

You are talking to a computer sales person about purchasing a new system for your office. You tell the sales person all your requirements who is adding everything up on your list. The sales person now hits you with a whopping $10,000. As soon as you are over your shock you are presented with another choice – a package deal for only $3,000. What a deal! What an easy choice to make. Of course, that is what they wanted to sell you in the first place.

Let's say you are going on a job interview and you are going to use the choice close set up. Arrange for two interviews, one immediately following the other. Have a friend go on the first appointment and have them intentionally screw up the interview. Then you go in, well prepared, on the second appointment for your interview and the choice becomes obvious.

If you think this sounds a little shady, consider this choice close set up used by undertakers. The undertaker will first show you a low budget, low price casket that is carefully positioned in a dark corner of the showroom. Then they show you the higher priced casket and point out all the benefits. Compared to the low end casket it is an easy choice to make.

What does this have to do with you?

The next time you present a product to a customer take two products instead of one. Take in an overpriced high end product along with the one you want to sell. Show them the over priced, high end product first. After they get over their shock, bring out the one you wanted to sell in the first place and it will seem like an easy choice.

Guarantee close

Before using the guarantee close you have to be sure your company or the manufacturer will go along with it. It is similar to a closing tactic called the "puppy dog close". The pet store owner tells the parents of the little boy to take the puppy home over the weekend and if they are not happy with it they can bring the dog back on Monday. Of course you know what will happen during the weekend and the dog will never come back. When using this close in a more professional setting you might tell the buyer to try the new coffee machine for thirty days and if they are not happy with it we will pick it up and reinstall the old one. Some companies have even gone so far as to buy out the existing supply of a competitor's product if they agree to try the new product for 30 days.

Time advantage

The time advantage creates a sense of urgency during the presentation. "While supply lasts" implies that there are several other sales people selling the same program and if you don't put your order in right now you might miss out. "Limited time only" implies that the price will soon go back to the book price. "Sale ends Friday" also creates the feeling of missing out on an opportunity. "One time offer" is designed to put pressure on to take advantage of the promotion now or miss out all together. "Longer shelf life" is also a way of taking advantage of time if the shorter shelf life of a competitor is causing a loss due to waste. "New inventory is higher" implies that the market has gone up and we are holding our price down until we sell out of our current stock.

Trial close

The trial close is designed to lower pressure by using the word "IF". If you decided to buy which portion or pack size would be best? If you decided to buy how many could you sell in a week? If you put this in stock would it benefit your customers? If you stocked this line for one year how much money would it save you?

These trial questions should be part of your presentation. The purpose is to see how close you are to the actual order in a low pressure way. Build test questions into presentation and use them often. The key is to start them with the trial word "IF".

"Ask a question" close

The ask a question close is based on the fact that it is sometimes hard for a customer to say yes, however, it is much easier to for them to say "No". The magic question to ask is this: "Is there any reason why we shouldn't go ahead with this?"

If your first attempt doesn't get the response you want - ask a second time. Wait a short period of time then ask again as if we were asking for the first time. The theory behind this close is the time it takes for a new idea or concept to take hold. It takes time for the mind to work and when we ask the first time there is a natural defense mechanism at work. However, after just a few minutes the buyers mind will start making mental associations and will have more information available to make the decision. Anybody can ask once and accept a negative response.

Doorknob close

The reason this is a "last resort close" is because we should try everything else first. After they refuse to buy, close your presentation, put everything in your brief case and act as if you have stopped trying. In some cases you can actually go to the door, stop, turn around as if you have left and returned as a friend instead of a sales person. This is designed to lower their guard. Then ask the question: "Where did I go wrong?" At this point look at your watch and make a commitment to stay 15 minutes longer. You will be amazed at the difference in the person you are trying to sell.

Silent close

The silent close is the most difficult to use because it seems so unnatural. The hardest thing for a sales person to do is to be quite for 30 or 45 seconds. When there is silence it almost seems like we are not doing our job, however, just the opposite is true. We have to give the buyer a chance to think things over and he can't do it if we are talking away. Keep in mind that the biggest complaint buyers have about sales people is that they talk too much. After the facts have been presented try and remember one thought: Whoever talks first loses.

The truth about closing

When a customer has made up their mind that they are going to buy, they buy, they do the closing.

From time to time you should try to discover just how much you have accomplished in transporting the person in front of you to a state where he or she sees themselves using what you have to offer to their advantage. This can be done with "qualifiers" put in the form of questions such as, "where do you plan to put this, Mr. Brown?"

The psychology of the "close" has been so talked about by sales experts that it has frightened more sales people than it has helped. When a person has made up their mind that they are going to make their imaginary picture a reality, then they do the closing, they buy, you don't sell them except to make it easy for them to sign an order.

You started to close the moment you decided to call for the appointment. You are closing all the way through the process.

As your presentation proceeds it should include steps which apparently fit into the running story but which actually are used by you to anticipate objections. The time to answer most objections is before they are brought up, during the presentation.

Here is the TRUTH about closing...

If you don't build rapport
YOU WILL NEVER CLOSE

If you don't get them talking
YOU WILL NEVER CLOSE

If you don't gain their trust
YOU WILL NEVER CLOSE

If you don't make a great presentation
YOU WILL NEVER CLOSE

If you don't overcome their objections
YOU WILL NEVER CLOSE

If you don't make it easy for them to buy
YOU WILL NEVER CLOSE

If you don't fit your product into their future
YOU WILL NEVER CLOSE

If you don't follow up on your promises
YOU WILL NEVER CLOSE

If you don't ask for the order
YOU WILL NEVER CLOSE

Usually people who have never had to go out and ACTUALLY MAKE A SALE think that selling is all about closing. Trying too hard to close without providing the rest of the program will turn off customers faster than anything else you do.

How you decide

Have you ever laughed at a joke that wasn't very funny, but everybody else laughed so you felt the obligation to laugh? Have you ever bought something based on the fact that it was the "best selling" or "fastest moving" item? Would the statement "4 out of 5 people surveyed recommend this product" influence your decision? How about "over two million copies sold" on the cover of a book? Would that make you feel more comfortable about your decision to buy it? If so, you are not alone.

People are highly influenced and persuaded by what others do.

I am the first customer to go through the car wash, yet the tip jar has 10 one-dollar bills folded in the jar. I am the first one in the bar and notice the bartenders tip jar already has several dollar bills in it. I am the first one to put money in the collection basket at church, yet I notice that there are already several 5 and 10-dollar bills in plain sight.

What does all this mean? It means that this concept works and it can work for you too. Here's how.

Everybody likes to think of himself or herself as a nonconformist – someone who does their own thing. You and I like to see ourselves as independent – until it comes time to make a decision – then we find out what everybody else is doing and what everybody else thinks – and conclude that they must be right – and make the decision that I am going to do the same thing.

Do you see the relevance to your business?

Let's say you are a new sales person calling on a potential account. Would you say; 'I am new and don't have any customers yet – will you take a chance and be the first?" If you were a seasoned sales person would you go into a potential customer and say; "We have great quality and excellent service?" No, you wouldn't want to say something like that because their response would be "so what." You would want to take the approach that the bartender, car wash, church, evangelical preacher and concert promoter took. You want to bring on your success stories, testimonials, references, people your prospect knows and a list of happy customers who are buying from you. You would want to put a little money in your tip jar to show that others are buying and they are happy. Why? To make them feel safe about their decision to buy from you.

We find out what everybody else is doing and what everybody else thinks – and conclude that they must be right – and make the decision that I am going to do the same thing. This is the best closing technique of all.

Closing on price

Only 15 percent of buyers change vendors based on a lower price. When your customer understands the value of your offer, price is seldom the real issue. Your customer has a problem to solve and is willing to part with hard-earned money to solve it.

When we are selling a new customer we must sell on something other than price. One of the big mistakes many sales people make is they over exaggerate their claims. They use such overworked phrases such as:

"We are number one..."

"We are the best in the business..."

"You can save big money with us..."

As soon as one of these statements is made a red flag goes up in the buyers mind. We have just "unsold" ourselves. They know immediately that we are not legitimately interested in them. To get them to buy from us we must present a strong case.

The buyer's single concern is their own interest. The buyer has three questions: "So what?", "What's in it for me?", and "Can you prove it?" Facts, figures, and precedents should continually enter into the presentation to justify statements. These facts make the buyer willing to accept you and your offer and make a change based on something other that price. Our goal is to weave the facts into the conversation that makes the customer understand the legitimacy of what we are selling. For example:

"Our program will increase your profits by 6% - here's how."

"This product line will cut your labor cost by 3% - I have the facts right here to prove what I'm saying."

This new marketing system will increase your sales by at least 5% - let me show you what I mean."

A sale is closed when the buyer agrees with our presentation. We are looking for buyer commitment. If you get a customers business based on price - your competitor will take it away from you based on price.

It is always to our advantage to support our sales presentation with backup evidence from impartial sources. Expert testimony is hard to challenge. Having back up information by a third party is a high standard of legitimacy to win their confidence.

After the close

Beware of the person who agrees to your price too quickly, they may plan on asking for more.

If the buyer agrees to your price too quickly there is usually a request that will be close behind.

"That price sounds pretty good, I will take 100 cases."

"By the way can I have special terms on that?"

Another customer might agree to the price right away and ask for same day or next day delivery. From a buyers perspective this is called the "add on."

Agree to the initial price and then as soon as the sales person starts ringing up their commission, drop the "add on" question. This is also an excellent strategy for you to use as a sales person. Once you have what you want in hand, there is a natural tendency to leave as fast as you can. Perhaps there is an unconscious fear that the customer will change their mind or cancel the order - just the opposite is true.

Once a person makes a decision, their mind works to reinforce the decision. By getting a small commitment first the buyer will start to justify the decision and it becomes easier, not harder, to add on additional items.

Why? Think about your own decision making process. Once you make a decision your mind does a search, similar to a computer doing a search for additional information. Your mind is looking for ways to justify the decision you just made.

Your customer's mind works the same way. This tactic is being used on you every time you buy a car. First the car sales person will get you to agree on color, then options, then an extended warranty, and before you know it you bought the car - one small piece at a time.

The last-minute add on involves throwing in an extra request (usually not so huge as to break the sale but big enough to hurt) at the final moment, just when you, the sales person, has put down your defenses and assumes you have a deal.

The add-on seems to go against a person's nature. "I got what I wanted, I better leave before he or she changes their mind."

To successfully use this tactic, stick around a while. If you are selling multiple items, sell the first one. Wait a few minutes, sell the second one. Wait a few more minutes, sell the third one, and so on. Give the buyers mind a chance to justify their decision.

Remember, they are thinking, "I bought the first one - I might as well buy the second one. I bought the second one - I might as well buy the third one." That is how little orders turn into big orders. It is like going into the grocery store and buying a chicken. I bought the chicken - I better buy the potatoes - the salad - the rolls - the desert - and before you know it your shopping cart if full.

Once you make a decision your mind does a search, similar to a computer doing a search for additional information. Your mind is looking for ways to justify the decision you just made.

Expect the sale

Do you go into each sales call with the HOPE of making a sale, but not necessarily expecting it so you won't be disappointed?

In a recent test researchers found out that if they put a blindfold over someone while they are eating, they eat less. Let's take this another step and ask ourselves this; what if all of a sudden you or I lost our memory and our sight at the same time? What if no one would tell us how old we were and we would have to guess?

What would you say?

Now let's take it another step and ask ourselves what if we were unable to remember any of our past failures and disappointments, but could only remember our successes. What if someone followed us around all week with a movie camera and edited out all the stupid stuff we did? At the end of the week they played everything we did right, every success regardless of how small it was and removed all the bloopers.

Now let's go one step further. Let's say that you are a researcher rather than a sales person. Your job is to do market research and find out why people buy or don't buy. Your success is not going to be determined by whether you make a sale on that particular call, but your success is going to be determined by doing the research.

You make the call expecting people to see you. You expect them to treat you with respect. You expect them to listen to you. You expect them to answer your questions. If the timing is right and what you are offering is the solution to their problem, you expect them to buy. If the timing is not right, or the solution is not a good fit, you would expect them not to buy.

At the end of the day when someone asked you how your day went, how would you answer? Would you say you were a success or a failure? No. You would say I talked to 15 people. Two of them were having problems and I was able to offer a solution. Ten of them were happy with what they were doing but agreed to have me come back at a specific time in the near future. Three of them had very closed minds and were not open to anything new regardless of how bad they needed it.

So instead of making the call as a typical sales person, make the call like a consultant would.

For example: "I am doing some research in the area to find out if our services would be beneficial. Do you mind if I ask you three questions and it will only take three minutes to answer?"

So, if we put a blindfold on you that filtered out the normal fear a person has when approaching a stranger while trying to sell them something, what's left? Confident expectations of doing the job. And the action will create hope, which comes from doing the details of the job exceptionally well. And when you do your job exceptionally well, it is impossible to be disappointed.

Knowing exactly what you want, expecting to get it and visualizing the outcome is effectively managing your confidence level. When you spend time planning your strategies you are creating a situation you desire. You have control over the outcome.

If you are not advancing towards your goal with the expectation of success, it is not the goal that is out of reach. It is the daily activities that need attention. The common denominator of all successful professional people is the same. THEY ALL EXPECT TO SUCCEED.

The common denominator of all unsuccessful sales people is the same. Deep down inside – THEY ALL EXPECT TO FAIL.

Look at a successful surgeon. When they operate on someone they have the positive expectation of success.

A lawyer is another good example. When they are addressing the jury they have the 100% positive expectation of convincing the jury to see things from his or her point of view.

A politician must have the expectation of success. If you interview several candidates running for the same office the night before election, they would all believe they won. If they lost this expectation of winning at any point during the campaign they would immediately be out of the race.

However, there is a difference.

Most professional people must go through several years of higher education before actually starting in their profession. All during these years the attitude of high expectations is slowly building day by day. Once they have invested in four, six or eight years of education they feel they have earned the right to expect success. And they have.

Compare that to the profession of sales. If you have never sold a thing in your life, have very little formal education and are looking for a job – you can start a career in sales tomorrow! The profession will welcome you with open arms no matter what your background, experience or education may or may not be.

In sales you have not had the day-by-day, year-by-year preparation that most professions have. You may go through a short company training program that pumps up your expectations to a high level, however, once you enter the real world, alone and unprepared for what's next, your expectations take a downward turn and things look different.

To succeed there has to be certain things in harmony. Your expectations and your goals must be equal. If your goals are too high or unrealistic you won't expect to reach them and you will see to it that you get what you expect.

Your goals must be clearly defined, realistic, reachable and most importantly APPROACHED WITH THE POSITIVE EXPECTATION OF SUCCESS.

Without the advantage of having four years of sales training before making your first sales call, you have to take a different approach. You have to teach yourself this important principle of selling – to expect success.

Closing: Ask for the order and get paid

I am able to ask for the order in a way that the customer feels good about spending their money with me. I am able to steer the sales process towards a predetermined objective that makes it easy for the customer to go forward and make the commitment. I have done such a good job of presenting my company, my offer and myself that the customer feels no pressure when it comes time to go forward. When I am working with a prospect that may take several visits to bring them all the way through the sales pipeline I have the specific objective clearly defined for each step of the process. I have done such a flawless job of bringing the sale to the point of the close or next step that the process seems smooth and natural.

My 4% improvement objective:

_____

_____

_____

_____

_____

_____

What the entire book series will do for you

Buying all 13 books is like buying a library of 13 powerful coaching sessions that will increase every skill necessary for generating business. Once you experience the seemingly effortless improvement you will understand why there is a picture of Ben Franklin on every 100 dollar bill.

You will learn how to improve relationships, improve management skills, be more productive, generate more customers, negotiate better contracts, open new accounts, earn more profits and create more sales! Results most people only dream about! If you are a sales professional or an entrepreneur this is the perfect program to boost your sales and increase your profits.

Ben Franklin's system

In our fast paced business and personal life today it has become increasingly difficult to set aside time for self development and improving your skills. With every spare minute taken up by reading blogs, logging on to Facebook, following people on Twitter, responding to text messages and emails and constantly talking on your cell phone, there seems to be little, if any, time left for learning new skills. Even the quiet time behind the wheel of your car is no longer available with satellite radio and cell phone coverage in every corner of the country.

Even though this seems like a new problem, distractions have been around forever. Two hundred years ago a man by the name of Ben Franklin had the same problem. He concluded that it was not a matter of distractions as much as a matter of focus. He set out to solve the problem and created the most effective system for self improvement ever invented.

Ben Franklin gives credit for all his success and accomplishments to the implementation of this system for the success he sought after. Despite being born into a poor family and only receiving two years of formal schooling, Ben Franklin became a successful printer, scientist, musician, author and one of the founding fathers of the United States. Ben Franklin is considered to have been one of the most persuasive and successful people in the history of the United States. He was a very skilled sales person, marketer, negotiator and copywriter. Skills that every business owner, professional person, manager and marketer should have.

In the year 1723, Ben Franklin, at the age of seventeen, arrived in Philadelphia without a penny to his name. At age 42, he retired, wealthy, the first self made millionaire in the country. Few people, before or since have ever been as successful as Benjamin Franklin. He gave credit for his many inventions and business successes to his system for self improvement he created when he was 20 years old.

The key to Franklin's success was his drive to constantly improve himself and accomplish his ambitions. In order to accomplish his goal, Franklin developed and committed himself to a personal improvement program that consisted of mastering 13 principles.

When he was seventy-nine years old, Benjamin Franklin wrote more about this idea than anything else that ever happened to him in his entire life. He felt that he owed all his success and happiness to this one thing. Franklin wrote: "I hope, therefore, that some of my descendants may follow the example and reap the benefit."

Since success is developed by performing small and seemingly insignificant acts, you can use this method by reading and putting into practice the 13 skills that will guarantee your success in sales with scientific certainty.

This program takes advantage of Franklin's system and applies it to improving your skills as a sales professional. This program will show you how to dominate your market by first dominating yourself. By focusing on the 13 skills that make up a highly effective and successful sales professional. As these skills are improved your results and sales increases will also show a dramatic improvement.

The goal of going through the program the first time is to increase each skill by only four percent. With the accomplishment of this small improvement in each skill or attitude your overall improvement will be 52%. Those are results most people only dream about. However, you can accomplish this by investing as little as 45 minutes once a week reading one book and then focusing on improving the single skill during the rest of the week. The second week by reading the second book and focusing on that single skill during the week and so on until all 13 weeks are completed.

You can write the single word on the back of your business card and tape it to your dash board as a reminder. You can put this one word on your smart phone as a reminder as well as on your email signature, your Facebook page or you can even have something worthwhile to tweet about. One word, one week, one skill, one "I am" statement, 4% improvement objective and your subconscious mind will receive the message through all the clutter and act on it.

After the first time through the process you can do as Ben Franklin suggests and go through the program a second, third and fourth time. Get your whole sales team on the same page at the same time and you will experience a whirlwind of new excitement and new business. Or get a like minded colleague and join forces with accountability and focus.

Achieve a 52% improvement

Using Franklin's scientific program for learning your objective is to improve 4% in each area over 13 weeks.

1. Attitude Define what you want and go after it.
2. Respect Earn respect-no more comfort zone.
3. Service Help customers build their business.
4. Urgency Be enthusiastic get things done now.
5. Confidence Remove restrictions and limitations.
6. Persistence Keep going and never give up.
7. Planning Get big results by setting big goals.
8. Questions Ask questions that make the sale.
9. Attention Get attention with irresistible offers.
10. Presenting Give reasons why they should buy.
11. Objections Remove every roadblock to the sale.
12. Closing Ask for the order and get paid.
13. Follow up Remove all hope for competitors.

About the author Bob Oros (BobOros.com),

Bob Oros has been a full time speaker and author since 1992 with over 2,000 speaking engagements in all 50 states and several international locations as well as the author of 21 books on sales. Prior to starting his speaking career, Bob served six years in the US Navy as a Communications Specialist and then worked his way from a street sales person to the position of National Sales Manager for a Fortune 200 company.

CSP Award: Bob was awarded the designation of Certified Speaking Professional (CSP) by the National Speakers Association and the International Federation for Professional Speakers. Fewer than 10% of all speakers worldwide qualify for this award.

PWA Member: Bob is a member of the Professional Writers Alliance.

www.ingramcontent.com/pod-product-compliance
Lightning Source LLC
Chambersburg PA
CBHW072258170526
45158CB00003BA/1101